Life through the Eyes of a Hurricane
Doggie-Dog!

To Jim &
Harley ~

Best Wishes
always!

♡
T. Spaine

Hurricane

Tracy A. Spaine

Strategic Book Publishing and Rights Co.

Strategic Book Publishing and Rights Co.
12620 FM 1960, Suite A4-507
Houston, TX 77065
www.sbpra.com

ISBN: 978-1-61204-269-5

Book Design: Judy Maenle

For my husband, Scott
Who captured my bruised and battered heart
and taught me to fully love again.

And my son, Nicholas
Who gave me a reason to live, to love,
to dream and to be.

"Dogs are not our whole life, but they make our lives whole."

—Roger Caras

Acknowledgments

First, I want to recognize my "growing up" family: my mom, Fannie Bess; my deceased dad, Robert Currier; my three brothers, Mike, Tom, and David Hampshire; and sister, Dawn Currier. I also recognize the plethora of nieces and nephews that have touched my life.

Although time and distance keep us apart, we can never deny our roots.

Kudos and hugs to Dr. Barbara Winters, Martha Gillis-Dellafield and Tanya Lentz; without you I would literally not be here on this Earth. Your commitment and dedication to my life was truly astonishing, which is why I am here able to do what I do. My heart and soul are yours to behold.

Mrs. Linda Stoner-Rish, wherever you are in this world—the very first person in high school I was brave enough to share my writing with—thank you for the encouragement!

I have always felt the terms 'family' and 'friends' are synonymous, which includes all of my other family that encompasses my friends from childhood, high school, and college. To the individuals that have shared in this journey called life from the multitude of teaching jobs in Ohio, Florida, and North Carolina, including my students from 30 years of teaching children with special needs.

Finally, within this final group, I'd be remiss if I left out my writer and blogging friends from my website: http://thinkingspot-tracy.blogspot.com/. You truly have taught me and shown acceptance within the writing community.

Because of you, I can now say, "I am a writer!"

Table of Contents

Introduction

Hello!

My name is Hurricane! And I'm a dog—

Wait a minute. Stop right there! As you turn that first piece of paper to begin reading my narrative, I bet you are expecting, well, some human's perspective of what they believe my life as a dog might entail, but I pose this question to you: do they really know what life holds for me and

my canine friends? Do they actually know how it feels to roll in a pile of dog doo-doo or a dead carcass on the side of the road? I bet not; because seriously, when is the last time THEY rolled in lifeless remains to mask their scent? Hah, I spot a dead frog on the pavement and dive my body right into that unpleasant fragrance—bombs away!

I know my human family can't fathom carrying the rich stench that clings to my fur, embedded by the pressure placed upon my body when I roll, twist, and turn.

They stand beside me and yell, "Gross, that is so disgusting!" or "Hurricane, STOP!" because they just can't identify with why it is I do the things I do.

I don't know why I take those actions, but when they bellow those harsh words, well, it injures my ego.

Honestly, despite the fact that it may be sickening, it IS natural behavior for us. Did you know that for our ancestors; wild dogs and wolves, this was instinctive conduct? Far be it from me to change our history!

Oh, I often get sidetracked, so if you'll excuse me I must refocus on my story and the purpose for such chronicles. As I was revealing to you, while most human's project they are on familiar terms with specific thoughts implanted in our craniums, I am obliged to disagree; certainly no disrespect intended.

Therefore, it is with this anthology of stories that I aim to set the record straight and provide a tell-all book about what the existence of a dog is *really* like. I'm also well aware this will be read by young and old alike, so I'll do my best to watch my language and not get too risqué.

So where to begin? Okay, you want to know about the title? No, I admit, it's not very original but what would you expect from me? I'm only a dog. I am a golden retriever, whatever that is because, like I alleged earlier, all I know is I'm a dog! I recognize this because on every occasion I am taken for walks in the 'hood, people pat me and tell me what a beautiful dog I am.

Hah, I wonder if they'd still tell me that if they knew I just turned over in a rotted corpse of a squirrel. Or at least I think it was a squirrel! Poor little guy must have met his heavenly maker pretty quickly by the looks of him.

I do know that Big Daddy (that's the dad in my human family, but I'll introduce my family more extensively as we pass through this journey collectively) also known as Big D, wasn't overjoyed with me but gosh, could you lighten up a bit, huh?

Anyway, before I get too engrossed I'll tell you I was born October 23, 2008 in Chapel Hill, North Carolina, which must be good because my family loves this college called University of North Carolina and presumably it's in Chapel Hill.

I'm a very logical thinker, so before I forget, let me first introduce you to my cast of characters, ah, I mean my human family. I already mentioned Big Daddy. Let's see, he's a runner and most often the one who takes me for my daily jaunts 'round the neighborhood, which is when I get to visit with all my friends.

He was a teacher at one time but now does something else. But this is probably why he's always trying to get me to learn new things, which I'm not really into. I like things simple. Big D calls me his "Doggie-Dog," among other names, and we love to romp and wrestle together. He's generally the first person I make an effort to wake at the crack of dawn, and even though he scolds me every now and then, the rewards of cuddle time definitely outweigh the risk.

Nee Nee is the mom and heaven only knows why she is called Nee Nee. When I was home with my doggie mom, I called her "mama." Regardless of the funny name given to her by Little D when he was small, she is a teacher of special kids and a writer. She also derives pleasure in taking photos of me and Little D, so it seems every moment of the day a camera is in front of my striking muzzle. She is not aware I sneak and use her stuff for the purpose of writing my memoirs. I certainly hope she doesn't find out anytime soon, so shhhh, please don't leak the secret for me! If she does happen to find out, I'll know it was YOU!

And Little D—ahhh, what can I say about my gentle-hearted, sweet young boy of eleven years? He is in reality the human whose idea it was to get me in the first place, so my heart is especially connected to Little Daddy. We are buddies and I treasure the times we scamper around the house chasing each other. We take pleasure in playing ball of any sort, and let's face it, I owe my life to Little D for choosing me. I know you'd like to hear of that now, but be patient and I'll get to it.

Like I was saying, my two-legged people sometimes articulate they'd like to trade places with me, but I really don't understand why. They say I have a trouble-free life but I have to be frank; I get quite offended when I hear that because, like I mentioned earlier, humans really don't value the life of a dog. I beg to disagree with them, and through my writings you will see that my life is anything BUT easy!

I'll do my best to slink on this button-filled contraption with lines from time to time and tell you accounts of life in my day-to-day existence. It will assure you that life can be somewhat difficult for a dog, such as the incident on the day before today.

Yesterday, Big Daddy was operating this machine across the carpets and I don't know what it is for, but it has a light on the front. When he rolls it toward me, the loud noise it makes—VROOM, VROOOOM—scares me half to death so I bark at it a lot to tell it to stay away. He says, "Hurricane!"—that's my name, by the way, and not some storm in the Atlantic, just so you know. "It's not going to hurt you!" but I run at it and try to bite it anyway because I can't be too sure!

Anyway, all of a sudden, it stopped! Big D leaned down, flipped the on-off switch, and jiggled at something in the wall and it wouldn't turn back on.

Dead! D-E-D dead! I'm so glad I finally killed it—for my family's sake. He sat on the floor, which is always my invitation to scramble into his lap. I've been doing that since I was a puppy and I get patted on my belly, around my ears, on top of my head—ohhh, it feels so good. I never want him to stop. When he does, I put my nose under his hand and swing it back up so he'll keep going. AHH-HAHHHH!! I could do this all day long! But this time, he just said, "Hurricane, outta my way!" OUCH, that hurts!

So I lay my head on the floor and give him my sad puppy dog look where I raise my eyebrows ever so slightly and stare at them . . . it gets them every time. Big D stroked my ears for just a few seconds more. I guess it is better than nothing!

Okay, so back to the apparatus with the glow on the front. Big D started taking it apart and OH MY GOSH! All my hair started coming out of it! When did my beautiful butterscotch hair fall out?

Big D kept saying over and over with each new bunch he extrapolated from that machine, "Hurricane, this is all your hair!"

I tell you, we sat there for twenty-five minutes while he pulled tufts of my fur out of every nook and cranny of that device and he put it all in the trash.

Boy, do I sure feel naked! Goodness, I do believe a hair transplant is in order!

Well, gotta go. I hear Nee Nee coming down the stairs so I better end this for now, but this isn't the last from me—I think I like this life!

Name Calling

Devil Dog? Is that what I heard, DEVIL DOG? But, but—I thought my name was Hurricane? I guess when I wake the family up at 3:00 in the morning my name changes, but what's a devil?

I know I have a dashing spirit, some mischievous moments, and I can be pretty reckless at times, but gosh, that's pretty harsh, wouldn't you say?

However, if I do have some devilish ways, I am serious when I utter, "I don't really mean to." I try to look at the numbers on the clock very carefully, but sometimes all those lines mix me up and when I see a five I can't remember if it's supposed to be at the front of a number or in the back; I just get so perplexed and confused.

I'm letting you know this because I got scolded this morning for waking up my family at 3:00. How was I supposed to know it was Saturday?

Gosh, I know I'm a smart dog but don't give me that much credit; such high expectations to live up to for a dog. Anyway, on any other morning when Nee Nee turns that box on beside *our* cradle—I say that because I claim that bed as mine too. Anyway, the container starts playing music when the numbers say 5-0-0. I want to help them get up and I know they are so happy to see me because I've been asleep all night, so I'm sure they have missed me, right?

So, with a huge levitation I bound on the bed and plunk myself right down in the middle between Big D and Nee Nee . . . but then they start saying, "You Devil Dog!"

Me? What did I do? I'm just helping . . .

At any rate, this morning—or was it nighttime? I just get bewildered and befuddled, but what I thought was a five was really a three and I took my usual dive onto the bed and plopped all 70 lbs on top of Big Daddy.

He protested and called me that D-name again, and so I wanted to make him pleased. Therefore, I gave him a couple of wet willies right in his ear with my tongue, sure enough to make him smile!

UH-OH, he didn't smile. He didn't even pat me and then Nee Nee groaned. I tried putting my head on her pillow to let her know I was sorry, but I guess in my excitement saliva dribbled out of my mouth, and when she fluffed the cushion under her cheek, well, you can only imagine what transpired next.

She humphed at me and said, "Hurricane, it's Saturday!" But gosh, even though they called me a bad name and grumbled, they DID get out of bed and have been up with me ever since . . . I don't know what this Saturday thing is all about, but to me it's just more time to play!

I love this life . . .

The 12-Step Program

Okay, I'm a lost and broken dog. I have a terrible confession: I have a sock fetish, which according to the dictionary means "an obsessive or unhealthy preoccupation or attachment with an object."

But there, I said it . . . and often heard that the first step in overcoming an addiction is to admit I have a problem. It is a terrible problem. I can't get enough socks, which is even more of a problem because they aren't my socks!

Well, they eventually become my socks because I chew and tear so many holes in them that no one can wear the foot coverings by time I'm done with them, but that's beside the point.

You see, they are my family's socks. I can't help it and I am so ashamed of myself. Whenever I see a sock in the laundry basket I have to go grab it, stretch it until I hear that priceless sound: ripping. AAHHHH, a sound of satisfaction! Tear it, shred it, and grate it; that is when they are at their best!

Even though Big D has tucked them deep into the toe of the shoe, I like to get into Big Daddy's running shoes. I stick my nose into the cavernous shoe until I can reach just a teensy-weensy thread and pull it out. Yeah, I know, the smell is pretty unpleasant and you'd think that would deter me, but I guess that indicates how desperate my dilemma is.

I've even been known to chase Little Daddy around the house when he's taking his shoes off so I can grab a sliver of the cloth and help in pulling it off his foot. If I do that, then at least the taste is in my mouth and there's a better chance I get to keep it since I put the entire sock in my jawbone and slobber all over it. They don't like to touch it when it is coated with dribble.

Then, I dash into my favorite upstairs hiding place: under the bed. I know, I know, I'm a big dog but I can still fit under the bed and no one comes in after me. The beauty of that is they know I have the upper hand, so they go to the cabinet in the bathroom to get a biscuit to entice me to come out. When I hear that box, I immediately go to my bed, the heck with the sock!—a quest for a later time and date. Besides, I have the best of both worlds: a biscuit AND the sock!

Yes, it is true. I go to great lengths to feed my addiction. I follow Nee Nee up the stairs biting at her heals until she gives them up, or until I trip her. Sorry, Nee Nee! Or, I stand on my hind legs at the washer and dryer searching for strays, and park myself politely at the dryer while clothes are being folded to quickly grab one that may fall on the floor. I'm getting pretty good at Snatch-and-Go's.

So while I've admitted my compulsion, I'm not ready to follow Step 6 OR Step 7 which states an individual is entirely ready to have God remove all these defects of character and humbly ask God to remove my shortcomings—ummm, should I? . . . NAAAHHHHH, I like socks too much and how else can I keep my family entertained by my antics?

I love this life . . .

DQ!

Lucky Me, Lucky me, we're going for ice cream!

If you couldn't tell, I love, Love, LOVE ice cream and always have since I was just a pup. I'm really not sure how it started but my family informed me that they've been going for "o'ceam" since Little Daddy was a small boy. The first time they took the little man for the delectable treat, my boy didn't like it. What was he thinking? How can you not love that rich, smooth, velvety lump of a cold refreshing treat? OH MY GOSH, YUM!!

This is what sets the process in motion. Someone in my family will say, "We're goin' for ice cream! Get in the car!" Well, you don't have to tell me twice. I practically knock anyone over who moves in my passageway and if someone is in my way?

"WATCH OUT!! Last one in is a rotten egg," and I want to tell you, I am typically NOT the last one in. I quickly claim the front seat and make Nee Nee sit in back. Hee Hee! She will plop down in the back and mumble something about *a spoiled rotten dog* under her breath.

Hey, I can't help it if she doesn't move any faster than that. Maybe if she had four legs she'd be in motion more hastily. So I glance back to make sure my family is in their place, belts all buckled, and off Big Daddy drives.

Just the thought of going to DQ gets me so energized I keep going back and forth, back and forth, between the front and the back. "Are we there yet?" I keep asking Nee Nee with my muzzle in her face, and then I head to the front and give Big Daddy a licky-licky on his cheek to advise him to hurry this bus up.

Little Daddy tells me, "Sit Still!" but I can't help it. I just want some ice cream. Let's see, I think I'll get my favorite, a vanilla cone. Yep, that's my favorite!

"Are we there yet?" and a licky-licky to you too, Nee Nee. I slurp at her ear as I walk by her to go to the back!

We finally arrive at DQ and I jump out of the van so excitedly and pull Big D across the parking lot while he gives me a stern warning, "Hurricane you gotta stop pulling!"

But I just can't help it, I'm so thrilled! I can taste that silky vanilla crème in my mouth as we speak.

I try to go into Dairy Queen but I'm reminded I can't go in; I have to wait outside. THIS IS SO NOT FAIR!

So I choose a table or bench outside, which is after I get done wandering toward anyone with the soft-frozen delicacy to see if anyone is willing to share. They all just pat me on the head and tell me how pretty I am, which is fine and dandy, but I prefer ice cream to kind words.

When Big D and Little D come out with the treats, I sit so nicely upon command and begin devouring my chilly delight. It is so luscious and mouth-watering that I have dribble running down my chin. Oh well, that's what Little Daddy's leg is for; just nestle up against him real close.

Ahhhh, this is such a glorious, heavenly weakness of mine I never want to be without ... oh no, is it all gone?

Nope, got the cone remaining so I grasp it gently with my front teeth as Big D releases his grasp, then I lay on my belly with the funnel between my two front paws to conclude my feast. Chomp, chomp ... and licking my chops afterward. YUM-MY! Then I sit patiently. Maybe if I manage to look very handsome someone will share with me!?

Oh well, even if they don't, Lucky me! I love this life ...

Emerald Isle

Is there a word that describes the feeling beyond excited? Like ecstatic? Ummm . . . maybe euphoric? Well, that's me today because I'm told we are heading back to the beach, Emerald Isle to be specific, and I LOVE, LOVE, LOVE the ocean!!!

In July when we were there, I didn't even wait for the car to be unpacked before I made a mad dash through the gate on the back deck toward the sparkling sapphire water. I turned around to glance back to see if my family was following me because I wanted them to enjoy the water too. They had their mad faces on so, of course, I kept on running down the beach as fast as my legs could carry me.

One little girl in a bright pink polka-dotted suit put her hands out trying to stop me so I would play, but I just turned my head her way to indicate "not now, gotta run to the end of the ocean . . . but I love your suit!"

But you know what? There IS no end to my ocean . . . it just kept going and going and going. OH NO, where was my family?

Well, as I turned back to search for them I remembered the water . . . ahhh, love the water except for the taste, BLECK! That's gross! I reminded myself to just keep my mouth shut so I wouldn't indulge in its bitterness. Hey, I think those waves are playing tag with me . . . it came and got my feet. "Okay, now you're in trouble!" I bark.

I run toward it and the waves chase me back and enfold my legs as if to say, "YOU'RE IT!"

We play this game until I tire of being "it" and my family finally discovers me. I'm wondering, "Hey guys, what took you so long?" They are so jubilant to be at the beach, they don't even reprimand me for my grand escape as we continue to stroll along the oceanside with the sand collecting deep in my paws.

I stop and dig my mitts into the sand and send it flailing back in a shower of particles until I plop down into the cool bed of ginger grains. I gaze up at my family to tell them, "AHHHHH, this is the life!"

Yeah, I remember those exceptional times and more, so it's with great exhilaration in my heart that I observe my family collecting their things so we can embark upon our journey. Nee Nee said something about the beach being tranquil and peaceful, an invitation for the stress to wash into the vast ocean, whatever that is, but to me, it's a never-ending playground of fun.

I love this life . . .

Hurricanes

I know, I know . . . I haven't been on the computer for well, in like forever, because it has taken me quite awhile to recover from our vacation to Emerald Isle and I'll tell you why. The beach was exquisite with all the opportunities to play chase the birds and lope with Little Daddy, search for crabbies in the sand, all my walks, and games of tag with the waves and WOW, what gigantic waves they were!

There was something about this expedition to the big blue bathtub I don't understand though. When we got to the ocean someone called "Hurricane Danielle" had been there so these scarlet flags hung on poles, blowing in the brisk breeze. Big Daddy said the streamers were there to tell us not to swim in the ocean. Well, what fun is that?

Besides, no one told me I could have met and played with Danielle, someone who shares MY name! If I had been there a couple days early, I could have joined in the fun with her. I bet she was pretty just like her name, but evidently I missed meeting her, DARN!

Anyway, I was amused from sun up 'till sundown. I took daybreak strolls on the beach with Big Daddy because he wakes up really early. I wonder if it has anything with me giving him licky-lickies on the face when just a hint of light peeks in the window? UMMMMM, anyway, he gets out of bed mumbling something about "Devil-Dog" . . . there he goes using that word again when I know my name is Hurricane.

So since he's awake, we go frolic on the seashore with the waves. Big D will locate a shell and fling it in the water and I will sprint after it. Once I ran too far in the water and this humungous wave appeared and took my feet right out from under me like I was being hog-tied, and then one more wave rumbled and landed right over my head. I had to close my mouth so I wouldn't drink any of that salt water, BLECK!

But really, WHEW, I couldn't find my feet for a split second! Big Daddy said Hurricane Danielle made the waves big. WOW, did she ever! She must have been really strong. I changed my mind; perhaps I didn't fancy meeting her after all. I'm really not an alpha-type dog, kinda chicken actually!

But like I was saying, I went for a jaunt every morning, then another in the afternoon. This was the time when Little D and I typically would amuse each other by participating in a game of chase. He would rush ahead of me into the waves and then shout to me to come get him. I'd get so excited sometimes I'd knock him down. I'm so sorry Little D, but I just love this!

Our third spree for the day was when that life-size ball in the sky was coming down just about to touch the dazzling sapphire water. My, that was sure a pretty part of the day. Being a dog, I'm not real good with my colors but I think there were yellows, reds, and oranges that streaked crossways through the sky, making a beautiful backdrop for that golden ball, but then the sphere would vanish and the heavens would get dim.

We'd park ourselves on the soft sand to gaze at the birds and watch the people. Often the people would come to a standstill before us, stroke my head and utter to my family, "He is such a beautiful dog!"

"Thank you very much!" I'd say in my mind because that's what my family always says to them. But then, it would get

too shadowy, and I would want to go into the beach house because, well, I'm afraid of the dark and the shapes the dusk makes, but don't tell everyone because it's kind of a secret.

At any rate, there were plenty of walks and times that the long strap that goes around my neck was taken off and I could just dart, dash and scurry about . . . AHHHHH, I love the blast of air and mist in my face and when it tickles my nose, it makes me sneeze! "Bless you!" they'd shout in my direction!

But just when I was having so much fun with the waves and the birds and all the strolls, on Thursday my family started to put all our things in bags and boxes and place them all in our van.

"What was going on? We can't leave yet because I'm still having fun!"

Little Daddy said, "Hurricane Earl is coming." Well, I know I didn't invite Hurricane Earl so why is he coming? I just don't understand all this use of my name. And if we didn't invite Earl, why does he have to be so mean and make us leave?

Nevertheless, Little D said something about a mandatory evacuation and so the flurry of activity continued. I was anxious they were going to depart, leaving me behind, so after a while all I really cared about was that they put ME in the van with all my treasures. *"Hey, Little D, don't forget my sock under that table! Now, where did I see my ball?"*

PHEW, they finally did situate me in the vehicle on top of my soft lamb's wool bed. However, I was so despondent and so miserable. I love my time at the beach, and I love the time with my family and I'm still wondering, *"Why did I never get to play with any of those other hurricanes?"*

An Empty House!

As complicated as it has been, I have adjusted to reality from our shortened vacation. I'm confident I like this vacation stuff though, because my people are home with me all day long and I adore my family being with me. I get this warm, cozy sentiment inside my belly that oozes up through my mouth, and I just have to give everyone wet willies whether they are fond of them or not. SLURP!!! SLURP!!!

"Hurricane, Stop!" they utter to me, but I make believe I don't hear a thing they are saying and carry on giving those licky-lickies I'm most famous for.

What's more, when we are all together in our humble abode, a scratch behind the ear or a stroke on the head is never far from my reach. All I have to do is lie in the middle of the floor with my nose down, take a deep breath, and let out this long loud S-I-G-H! Whoever is closest will look at me and when I have their full attention, I arch my eyebrows just a touch that gives me those sad puppy dog eyes and know by now, I got them right in the heart. So they park themselves close beside me on the floor and that is my invitation to roll over on my back to get my belly stroked or my ears rubbed; ahhhh, now THAT is heaven! Oh yeah, Little Daddy, "Keep on caressing those ears . . . that is the best!"

Life was going along just dandy until Monday morning.

What? Why is everyone getting into the shower and putting their ironed clothes on? When they dress in their ironed clothes that can only mean one thing: they are, OH-NO, leaving?! I despise when they leave given that I don't like being alone. An empty house has got to be as bad as, well, having one's personals removed, if you know what I mean!

But sadly, they all get their things and Little D gets a bone out of the pantry. Hah, no fair, feeding me to take my mind off things. But hey, if you insist!

The noises on the exterior of my window panic me and I slink through the house and investigate; however, my family is nowhere in sight. I get so frightened when the sounds outside come to visit.

"Tchrring" what in the world was that shrill sound? I crouch down on my belly and take notice of the "tchrring" again out the back window. Oh my, I sure wish Big Daddy was here to protect me . . .

"Lay low!" I tell myself so no one will see me. All of a sudden, I spot Mr. Squirrel sitting on the deck railing scratching the house as he gazes deep into my eyes because he knows . . .

He KNOWS I am scared! *"ARRGHH, where is my family?"* Okay, time to go under Big D and Nee Nee's bed to hide from the turmoil.

When the noises stop I creep out, keeping tuned in to my surroundings. Once the coast is clear, I charge downstairs and go into my living room to sneak onto the sofa, but don't tell anyone because I'm not supposed to be on the couch. I'm sure my humans will forgive me once they know how frightened I've been.

After what seems like forever, I hear the garage door release. UH-OH, busted . . . I hop down and rejoice by wagging my tail and dancing when Little D comes bee-bopping around the corner. He greets me in such a joyful voice that all the chilling noises vanish from memory.

Whew, Little D, so delighted you're home, let's go outside and potty! I love this life . . .

My New Friend

No, we didn't get another darling to live at our address with me, although I'd really like a companion. As you know, I don't like staying home by myself so having a cohort would be a wonderful welcome. I'd never be lonely and I wouldn't be scared of the shadowy figures on the walls. I also wouldn't feel it necessary to hide behind the door when my family comes home since a friend would give me just the courage I'd need to greet them.

You see, the last couple days or so when my family has taken me for my walk in the morning—which is one of my favorite times during the day—I love to see, or shall I say *smell* all of my friends who have come before me.

I sniff the mailbox post, dribble a little bit of my scent onto it, then go over to the bush: sniff, dribble, repeat, sniff, dribble, repeat . . . and oh, mustn't forget that giant tree over there . . . sniff, dribble, repeat . . .

Big Daddy gets so impatient with me at times and asserts, "Hurricane, come on!" in this fussy, firm voice as he yanks on that thing around my neck . . .

"Gosh, I'm sorry but a dog has to do what a dog has to do!" Ahh, my friend Ripley was through here earlier, or was that last night's smell?

I believe that was Rex. "Rex, my man, you da dog!" And can't forget Max. Max, where have you been buddy? I haven't smelled you in so long . . . EEWWW, got a little too close to that one and it went right up my nose, AAA-CHOOO!

"God Bless me!"

Anyway, as I was saying about my new friend, Nee Nee and I started down the darkened street and what did I see? Right in front of me was this diminutive gray kitty. Yes, I know I'm a dog and should want nothing more than to chase that feline right out of my neighborhood, but there was something special about this cat from the moment I laid eyes on her. She, well I don't actually know if it was a he or she because I'm not real good at telling these things, especially on a cat, but let's say for the purpose of my story, it was a she.

She bravely pranced right up to me, tucked her chin to her chest, and rubbed her ears against my legs. Really?

Awww, little kitty, you are pretty daring; there are so many dogs who would devour you for breakfast. But this petite fluff ball with an ashen diamond of fur gracing her neckline kept stroking beneath my tuft of ruff. Oh, she was as sweet as my DQ ice cream, and you know how much I love my frozen treat. She was brushing up against me, back and forth, back and forth. I was mesmerized by her tenderness, her fearlessness, and her devotion to me as a stranger.

Nee Nee hesitated and considered us with softened eyes. I wanted to inquire if we could take her home since she was obviously fond of me. Geez, we have so much love to share at our residence! Instead, we hedged forward and left the miniscule ball of fur sitting in the middle of the road following us with her eyes.

As we sauntered away, I threw a glance back and murmured, "Goodbye, little friend, I hope to see you tomorrow."

I love this life . . . and my new little friend.

A New Toy!

YIPPPEEEE!!! I got a package in the mail on Saturday!

Well, okay, it wasn't for me but for my boy, Little Daddy. Yet I have this firm belief that EVERYTHING in this house is mine! At any rate, here he comes, racing into the house saying he got a present from BarbPat.

"OHHHH, I like presents!" although I never heard of BarbPat, but if it makes him thrilled then it's okay by me!

"BarbPat were our neighbors when we lived in Ohio," Little D advised me.

BarbPat? I created this quizzical look on my mug and cocked my cranium to one side. This generally tells my family I'm perplexed, which seems to happen a lot! These two-legged humans sure know how to muddle very simple things.

In any case, BarbPat is actually two people, Barb AND Pat, he was explaining; but when he was a little tyke, he shoved the words together and just called them both by one name, BarbPat—whatever! Works for me if it works for him!

So as I was saying, they sent this parcel to Little D and he was as blissful as a dog peeing on a post. He spied an opening and ripped until the contents splattered out onto the table.

I sniffed it before my eyes caught a glimpse of my treasure. WOW! For me? BarbPat don't even know me and they mailed me a toy? How cool is that?

I am crazy about my toys . . . I love to tug, shake and squeak every single one of them, so much amusement! But my latest toy was da bomb! It was a crimson nylon, sculpted bone packed with fluff and a squeaker; those are preferred! I find it irresistible to sink my teeth into my playthings so I can listen to that reverberating peep . . . PEEEP!!! An added trendy article, attached to one end was a knotted braid of scarlet, white, and black rope so Little D could grasp onto one end and I could heave with the other.

I raise my hind quarters into the air and unfalteringly dig my toenails into the mushroom-colored floor covering and give it all my muscle, PUUULLLLL! Whenever we do that, I haul him across the room. I love the sound of Little D's laughter! That's one of the finest parts of being a dog.

My best part is EVERY part, but Little D considers the most excellent element to be the Ohio State University insignia monogrammed on the bone and words that describe me perfectly: "GUARD DOG"! YEP! Yep, that's me . . . I ALWAYS guard and protect my family!

I love this life . . . AND new toys! Come on, Little D, let's play!

Whatever Do You Call It?

SQEEEEEEAKK!!!

Oh Little Daddy, Heaven's to Betsy, what ARE you doing?

SQEEEEEEEAKK!!!

Whatever that is, you are piercing my ears. Don't you realize that we dogs have incredibly sensitive ears? It sounds like you are strangling a chicken!

WHEW! Every nighttime, Little D unlatches this carbon box and digs out sections of ebony, circular pieces of something with gold buttons. He places a wooden something or other into a pointed piece that goes into his mouth and then he blows—

EEEGADSSS! I admit he is getting better, but goodness gracious. Every so often this throbbing, wicked screech comes blaring out of the metal contraption.

He works very hard to make beautiful noise escape through its chambers, but when he breaks a "reed" as he calls it, the black wood bellows and clamors like a wounded wolf on the prairie.

In truth, I do want to be of assistance to him because he gets so frustrated, so I offer a licky-licky on his arm as he's playing but he shrugs it off. Hey, that's not nice, Little D. I'm only trying to help.

Sometimes while he is sitting on his stool, papers in place—*music* he calls it—I rest my chin on his knee, stretching my eyes as far as they will go with little movement of the head so I can gaze into his concentration. Good, Little D. I try to applaud his efforts because when he isn't persuading the deafening sounds, it is rather lovely.

"Keep practicing, Nicholas, you're getting it!" says Nee Nee as she encourages him night by night to practice his clarinet. Ahhh, so that's what it is, a clarinet! Well, that's divine, Little D, just exquisite.

Little D works awfully hard, and the more he plays, the fewer times I have to cover my ears with my paws, which I know hurts his feelings.

I want to keep him in my eyesight, so I position myself in the hallway and let out a big *SIGH* to show my support, although he thinks I'm bored. But I'm not; the sound IS showing improvement every evening. My most beloved song is "Mary Had a Little Lamb." Personally, I think the title should be changed to "Mary Had a Little Dog" . . . but anyway, this song always puts me into a little snooze after dinner.

I love this life . . . and ahhh, the syrupy noise of music! ZZZZZ*zzzzz* . . .

Bath Day!

UH-OH!!!

I knew I was in a dilemma when my family lured me into the lavatory with a biscuit and then proceeded to fasten the door, click . . .

UGH, there was no escape! Big D turned on the shower. "Doomed!" I say. At least they afforded me the courtesy to allow me to finish my biscuit before they shoved me in that plastic box with the water that streams out of a metal tube.

I tried to sneak my way out by going behind Nee Nee and laying up against her as if to say, "Please Nee Nee, don't make me take a bath today . . . perhaps tomorrow!" But Nee Nee threw me under the bus and detached herself, so I was left unprotected.

Betrayed, I sneaked to Little D and gazed pleadingly into his eyes, "I'll take a bath later, Little D! Isn't that what you always say to get out of something . . . or was it, in a few minutes?" He looked at me straight in the eyes and informed me I smelled, so it had to be today.

I SMELL??? Well, no one told me that.

I SMELL?? I have a stench???? OH MY, I am so embarrassed, how could they not tell me? Really? Did all my friends I greeted on my walk this daybreak think that? Oh Lord, how will I ever face them again? I'm almost sure I used my Doggie Deodorant this morning.

As self-conscious as I was, I tried the "sad puppy dog" look, which really wasn't far from the truth, so I plopped down on the bathroom floor amidst all their echoes of demands and encouragement, and put my head between my outstretched paws and peeked at them. I raised one eyebrow to try as best as I could to give the impression of being pitiful, which I think was pretty successful because Big D approached, parked beside me, and started stroking my ears—SUCKER!

Then he calmly said, "Come on, Hurricane, you won't be so itchy after you've had your bath!" Well, he did have a point. I have been Mr. Itchy Scratchy lately.

Okay, so I summoned the courage to toddle pathetically toward the shower box with my head hung low and averted the gazes of my family, trying to invite all the sympathy I could muster. I know, I know, I love the ocean waters and enter quite readily, but that IS on my terms, understand?

I longingly want to pretend I possess a tad bit of control here. Big D pushes me toward the spraying water by shoving me in the rump. Geez, have a little compassion for a guy. So I take the plunge, so to speak, and step into the synthetic room. Big D sprays me with the tepid water and we continue through the process of getting "the stink" out of me, and although it really does feel refreshing, I don't want to let on that I feel like a million bucks.

Ahhh, I really love this toweling off. "Yeah, Big D, don't forget the belly!" Ooooohhhh! I perform a first-class shake and everyone takes cover.

"Hurricane!" they yell.

Well golly gee, what do you expect! Then the bathroom door releases and I sprint like a banshee all the way through the house, and each person steers clear while I race up and down the stairs, and in and out of each room. That is, until I settle on the bed with my family. "That wasn't so bad now, was it, Hurricane?"

It truly wasn't, especially when we all end up on the bed together. They whisper sweet nothings to me and caress my sodden coat, anything to comfort my ego!

Ahhhh, I love this life . . .

Auf Wiedersehen

I bet you don't know what those big words mean do you?

Well, I have to be honest and inform you I didn't know either until I *googled* it on the computer. The computer sure is a fascinating thing! When I first saw the words, I actually thought it was what dogs do: "ARF!"

But really, it translates into 'good-bye for now' in German, which is necessary to say since Nee Nee—that's my mom if you didn't know—she told me I couldn't write on her blog anymore. Can you believe she is cutting me off?

Sniff . . . sniff . . .

I have very mixed feelings about this latest development because, you see, from the moment I first crept onto the workstation with all these buttons with the multitude of shapes, well, I have to say I'm pretty proud of my efforts.

Besides, I take such delight in writing about my happenings, experiences, and this thing called life. The marks on the paper made me as free as a dog running in an open field. It just felt brilliant, you know?

Golly, there was so much I wanted to tell you all too; my first girl, Sadie, well, she was really my only girl and my children, bet you didn't know I had six pups, did you? I also wanted to tell you about how I chose my family, the place I was born, and oh, there was this time I snuck into the dryer—that was pretty funny!

What's more, I once had two kitty-brothers; Ginger Roozer and Tigger Magoo . . . ahhh, those memories make me smile and I positively miss those two rascals.

Nevertheless, it's DONE! KAPUT!

Momentarily ceased!

Evidently, Nee Nee sent my stories to a literary agent to see if they have potential, whatever that is . . . and to see if they liked the material enough to publish it into a hardback. When she received a response the other day confirming they would like to work with us, clearly that was what sparked the end of placing my stories onto our blog . . . uhh, I mean *her* blog.

She talked about opportunities and stuff I definitely do not understand, but I have to trust that she knows best. Did you ever hear the phrase "mama knows best"? Although I must tell you, I sure will miss sharing my script with you through this medium.

I still love this life . . . and Auf Wiedersehen, ARF!

Meet the Press!

I was reprimanded the other day for performing a mammoth breakout. Despite the results, it was actually quite exhilarating!

You see, when that happens I scurry out the entrance and race three houses down the road to see my buddy Diesel. If he's outside, we have the most excellent time doin' what dogs do best: rompin' and playin' and, of course, sniffin' and slobberin' all over each other.

"Diesel, you got drool running down your chin there, buddy! Wipe that off, man!"

I don't mean any disrespect, but we also chuckle at how crazy our owners get when they try to grab us. Hah! We're much quicker than they are; when we zig, they zag and when we zag, they zig. It really is quite comical to observe. All the while they are bellowing, "Hurricane, GET over here right now!"

"Diesel, you better stop, I'm telling you!"

Instead of listening, I throw out a comment, "Can't come right now, Big Daddy, havin' fun with my bro' Diesel!"

While I'm messin' around, little did I know that Big D stomped to the house to gather a rolled-up newspaper. So I saw him only as he approached me and as slapped it against his palm while using his gigantic voice, **"Hurricane! COME!"**

UH OH!!!

I immediately crouch down and place my head on the grass and give him those sad puppy dog eyes. "Is it working yet? Does he feel sorry for me?" I wonder.

I summon my pride following the reprimand and sullenly follow Big D back to our dwelling, head down, tail between my legs, and slinking all the way—you know the routine.

Rather than speculating how I was going to suck up and beg for forgiveness, my mind went to the point in time I was initially introduced to "The Press"! I was just a youngster. I didn't know any better, really I didn't. My family used the rolled-up newspaper to train me, which meant nothing more to me than instilling the fear of God to do exactly what they wanted me to do.

And you know what? It worked! That object scares me to death—I quiver in my shoes, well, my paws—just thinking about it.

CRACK! Just the thud of it sends shivers down my furry spine.

Anyway back to my memory . . . they all got in their vehicles at daybreak and traveled to wherever they travel to when they leave me all alone in this shadow-filled place.

I just got bored and went searching for something to occupy my time when I spotted it.

AHHHH! . . . the stick! *Meet-the-Press,* as they fondly named it.

But every time I even think of getting into mischief, that rod makes *me* think twice. So you know what I did? I attacked my fear head on!

I set my fears aside and grabbed that baton composed of newsprint and scratched at it, ripped it, tore it, and pulled it to shreds.

When I was done with that thing, it wasn't gonna hurt or scare no one ever again, namely *ME!*

It was now in a million tiny pieces all over the living room floor!

And the kitchen floor and the dining room floor. Ahhh, how I loved running end to end, the miniature bits taking flight throughout the house; it was actually very pretty. I was quite delighted with myself!

So imagine my surprise when Big D appeared with yet another Meet-the-Press club; I thought I destroyed that item.

Oh, cripes! I guess what they say is true; do the crime, pay the time? I speculate I'll just have to do another "search and seizure" tomorrow. They'll be so proud!

Even in the face of a scolding, I love this life . . .

Tears

Nee Nee cried the other day.

While I've never been instructed on the specifics of human tears since we dogs don't shed them, I knew in my heart it was because she was so sad. WE may not cry, but I know I am capable of feeling intense sadness, like when my kitty-brother Ginger Roozer died. I'll be sure to tell you that story a bit later.

So when I saw the droplets flow from her eyes, I went to her and licked the water from her cheeks and snuggled up next to her to let her know she wasn't alone. She was lying on the bed, propped by pillows and had a book in her hands. I wonder if what she was reading was the foundation of her sadness.

Well, when something makes me sad I try to escape from it, but Nee Nee kept going back to the book. The tears kept streaming and while I didn't mind, she held me close and had such a stronghold on me.

Nee Nee, I can't breathe . . .

. . . there, that's better.

She whispered to me, "Oh Hurricane, we love you so much!" How can that make her cry? I don't understand.

She finally put words to her weeping and relayed the tale of what she was reading *The Art of Racing in the Rain* written by Garth Stein. She said it was about the relationship between a man and his dog. Hey, that's me and my family!

I'll do my best to explain what I heard through her tears. A man and his dog, Enzo were best friends. The man experiences some very difficult times, and the dog was the source that stood by his friend. The dog was very old, encountered troubles with his belly, and suffered from hip dysplasia. The dog took his last breath in the arms of his most loyal human.

"Oh Nee Nee, that makes me so sad . . . please don't ever leave me!" I whisper as I place my muzzle gently upon her lap.

But really, I know she's thinking about me. Maybe she is thinking of my kitty-brother, Tigger Magoo. We had to endure the torment of having him "put to sleep," as they told me, but I know it really means that my friend and brother died. It makes my heart feel sad remembering the awesome times we shared.

Well, I thought they were grand, but perchance since he was the one always being chased, possibly he didn't think they were so wonderful. But I kind of think he liked the interaction, or he wouldn't have encouraged the pursuit by walking in front of me flicking his tail in my face to let me know of his presence.

Humans seem to be surrounded by death because I hear Nee Nee and Big Daddy frequently talk about people they know in their lives who have died. It is usually followed by a shaking of their head while saying, "It's very sad, but that's why we have to live our life the best we can every day!"

I couldn't agree more, which is why I licked those tears streaming from Nee Nee's face and snuggled right close with my head on her shoulder. I hoped she understood these nonverbal signals meant especially for her.

What I imagine is we only have one life to live well and to touch each other through our hearts, our minds, and our souls. It seems if we do our ultimate best to love and treasure each minute of the day, then perhaps we can let go of our last breath knowing we lived it to the best of our ability.

I've often said I'm just a dog so I don't know a great deal about this human world, but I do know that I am most happy when I greet each person I love with exuberance and lots of licky-lickies. I adore when my ears are stroked and roll over to get my belly rubbed. I take good care of myself with plenty of walks about my 'hood, daily naps, and I don't make a piggy of myself at mealtimes . . . well, at least I try not to.

I end each day with my favorite treat and lots of cuddle time, so Nee Nee, I will be around a long time. Please, you won't have to be sad and weep tears for me. I'll take good care of you all. Remember, I'm man's best friend. I love this life . . .

Happy Birthday to Me!

Happy Birthday to me, YEAH, baby, let's sing it!

Today is my birthday and I am two years old, so my family tells me.

As a dog it truly doesn't mean much to me, but hey, it seems to mean a lot to them. When they greeted me this morning, they were all gushy and conversed to me in that sweet, syrupy voice that makes me feel so warm inside. They also alleged they were taking me to DQ for ice cream, and I indisputably won't turn down that offer.

Although my memories are scattered and somewhat fuzzy, within my mind I went back to that tiny shanty located down a long gravel road in Chapel Hill where I first entered this world.

It was a crisp fall day with the crimson leaves turning cartwheels across the brunette grass. Maybe that is why the cool days provide a bounce to my step.

Anyway, my mama gave birth to eight slender fur balls coated in clear thin sacs, which is what we looked like when we first arrived. EIGHT! Can you imagine?! Eeegads! Poor Mama!

Well, I was only with Mama and my seven siblings for eight short weeks until my new family came to take me to the place I now call home. I'll tell you how that all came to be at another time, but for now the focus is on my mama since I couldn't have a birthday if I didn't have a mama.

Pitiful Mama, first she endured the labor and delivery of us, which Nee Nee told me is enough pain to cripple a bodybuilder, but then we all came out mewling, and gosh, imagine that from eight of us. I'm sure we got on her very last nerve. I wonder if Mama thought we were cute despite the throbbing pain we caused!

Well, she tolerated that pain-staking experience as well as us little ones attaching ourselves to her teats to give us nourishment only a mama can offer . . . awww, I love my mama! I adore the memories I carry within of our life together even though I wasn't with her for very long. She was never able to catch a break as my brothers and sisters and I wrestled and toddled on top of her, each barking and growling, trying to establish pecking order. Sometimes she'd have to rumble, snarl, or nip to teach us manners and acceptable behaviors, but we probably deserved it.

Like I said, I don't recall a great deal but I do know that some of my most endearing qualities were established early on by my mama. So at the age of two, I continue to be a cuddle-bug and crave warm embraces from my family. My heart is soft, which I think means it really hurts my feelings to be hollered at and scolded. My loyalty and care is plentiful for my family and so is my friendliness and love for the world around me, including anybody who wants to talk to me and give me pats.

So as my birthday unfolds, I will hold close to my heart treasured memories of my mama.

Now, let's go get that ice cream!

Ahhhh, I love this life . . .

A Trip to the Mountains!

Let me tell you how programmed I am. Whenever I see the suitcases come out of the closet and my family begins putting their stuff into those bags, well, I just assume we are going to the ocean.

So imagine my excitement when I saw my family rummaging around, talking about what they should bring and if they'll need this item or that one.

I could NOT wait!!

In fact, I even wanted to do the dance, "I'm goin' to the ocean, goin' to the ocean!"

I had this incredible desire to sing it at the top of my lungs, but I showed some restraint because I *am* two years old now, you know.

I have to be honest, though, and tell you I was slightly concerned since I didn't see them gathering any of my belongings, so I stayed real close. One time, Big D said, "Hurricane, you gotta move out of my way!"

Geez Big D, just stick a knife in my heart would you? I plopped down in the middle of the kitchen and managed a hefty sigh so if they had any inkling of forgetting me, they'd have to trip over me before they'd run off leaving me.

The gear was packed in the van and, whew, FINALLY they put my accoutrements in the back and ordered the directions to climb aboard! They don't realize how nervous I was becoming. I thought I might have a panic attack! But off we went! Driving, driving, driving . . .

"Geez Lousie, Big D, this doesn't seem like the way to the ocean," I wanted to throw his way, but he was getting grumbly about all the traffic, so I kept my thoughts to myself and peered out the window. Gosh, the aroma revealed we were just not in the right place, but I kept watching and waiting.

I couldn't find the vast, indigo swimming pool, but what a striking sight! It looked exactly like the multicolored gumdrops Little D likes to munch on. There was a stunning display of butterscotch, ruby, and gold swiped across the painter's palette.

"Wow! Big D, this is a dazzling portrait by nature. I can see why you brought me here."

It sure is a delight watching the leaves perform belly flops across the road before lying in their final resting place, creating a multicolored carpet. Wherever this place is we are traveling through is certainly a sight to behold. The soaring landforms reach out to God with their peaks and summits. And will you look at that? The billowy puffs of clouds are bending to greet them.

I hang onto Little D as we snake our way through the winding roads, being tossed like corn in a popper. I am filled with awe as we reach our sleeping destination among the stark and naked branches high up in the altitude.

"Nee Nee, why do my ears pop?" I ask and recognize there are so many questions I have as a dog. I shake my head forcefully to escape the bursts loose that are exploding in my ears.

"Let's go!" announces Big D. My family takes our belongings from the van and deposits them into the dwelling. We spend the days doing such vastly different activities than we do at the alluring body of water I find so irresistible, but fun and pleasurable nonetheless.

Who am I kidding by saying *we*? I realize I am JUST a dog, but they unloaded the vehicle and off they went on their merry way; they ate lunch and they panned for gems, which certainly does sound appealing! They had a stopover at Mast General Store and visited the countryside searching for firewood and trinkets.

All the while, they left me in a strange new place, which made me feel very gloomy and grumpy needless to say.

However, after their homecoming we had a divine time. We built a warm blaze in a cement slab, and I got to lend a hand eating the puffy marshmallows we roasted over the crackling flames.

"Hey, I'm eating the clouds we saw on our way here!" and boy, were they certainly scrumptious! We cuddled with blankets by the glow and drifted into a restful slumber.

The next day my family and I climbed atop one of those vibrant peaks that reach the heavens, and oh goodness, it was so dazzling!

Plus, I received so many pats and strokes from strangers who considered me so appealing; there were "ooohhhs and awwws," which made me quite cheerful! We captured photographs high atop those summits.

"Cheese," the photographer would request as I made an effort to give my finest grin.

But I have to be truthful; while the mountains were magnificent, my preferred place of travel continues to be the ocean. However, I think ANY time spent with my family is noteworthy and extraordinary.

I love this life . . .

Acceptance

I guess you could say I was adopted. I have a mama but she didn't keep me when I was born into her litter. I wonder if she kept any of us.

After I was born I stayed with my mama and seven siblings for eight weeks. She took such good care of us even though we were all little scalawags; suckling and hanging from her teats, as well as yipping, barking, snorting, and whining to keep her awake at night.

Poor Mama, we'd romp and play right on top of her and she was so kind when she'd just lay there and allow us to do that. One time my sister was foolin' around, wrestling with my brother, and when she tried to nip his tail instead she bit Mama on the tip of her ear.

Mama startled from her nap and scolded her, "Young lady, what do you think you are doing?" Goodness ... Mama, don't be mad, but I think we took Mama to Wit's End, wherever that is.

Anyway, back to the adoption. I looked it up in the dictionary because I wasn't quite sure the definition of this large word. What I discovered is it means "a voluntary acceptance of a child of other parents to be as one's own child, usually with legal confirmation."

So I guess what that means is my mama gave birth to me, and my boy and his family took me in to be their family. It was mentioned that I have AKC papers, so do you think it means I'm legal? I certainly hope so.

Those are the bits and pieces that actually don't matter, at least to me it doesn't. But what does matter is how MY adoption came about. You see, since there were eight of us and Mama really couldn't afford to take care of us, the two-legged ones that owned Mama invited all these strangers to come to our modest shack to peek at us and choose one to take home.

That sounds rather impersonal, doesn't it? But that's exactly how it happened. A fresh batch of human folk would arrive and ask to see my litter-mates and me, so we were all brought out of the back room and carried into the front space.

Then they played "pick and choose" like we were apples in a barrel; if there was a bruise or flaw, put it back and check out the next one. I always felt a stream of sorrow whenever a human would come, root through the goods, then leave. I became distraught when I was not given a ribbon around my neck signifying I was chosen by a family.

Then one day, a little boy entered the room with his mom, and the two-legged human came to get the four of us not chosen thus far. The little boy sat on the floor while my brothers and sister romped around the room—I'm sure to avoid getting their hearts broken once again by hoping they'd be "the chosen one."

I walked over to that boy and attempted to crawl into his lap. He so gently picked me up and positioned me on his legs. For some unknown reason, I felt very safe so I curled into a little ball in the crux of his arm and promptly drifted into sleep.

I dozed and woke to hear murmurs of the human voice saying, "Nee Nee, this one has chosen me. I think he's the one!"

Nee Nee replied to the boy and asked, "Are you sure?"

"Yeah, I think Dad and I should come back tomorrow so he can tell me what he thinks."

I liked the sound of those words, but suddenly, I was taken to my mama in a cheerless state. I truly had the notion that this boy was THE ONE!

But he left and no ribbon was placed around my neck. Alone yet again!

I currently wanted to sleep although my sister, who had been singled out, wanted to chatter all about her human. "Go away, Sis, we'll talk tomorrow," I said to her, hoping I could steer clear of her excitement. I slept the hours of darkness with a heavy heart.

The next break of day, the talk with my kinfolk focused on the humans who would be taking them home in a few weeks. I tried to act as if I was joyful for them, I really did. Mama was in high spirits since she was convinced her pups would make her proud.

We no longer depended on Mama for her milk but were sloppily eating kibble. I finished my breakfast and Mama was giving me a spit-bath. "Awww Mama, do you have to do that?" I asked, when all of a sudden, the human worker scooped me in her arms and took me into the front room.

Then I saw the boy standing in the front room.

"MY BOY!" I exclaimed to myself.

"Oh please, oh please, oh please choose me!"

He **had** come back with his papa just like he said he would, and they were now sitting on the floorboards with me. The boy's papa picked me up and held me to his nose, which I responded to with a licky-licky on his nose; that made the boy laugh!

Then when my boy was holding me, I tugged on the metal thingamajig of his jacket and he giggled. Oh, how I loved that sound! He held me close to his cheek. I could smell his sweet skin and held such a strong desire to be singled out as special. I could have stayed in his arms forever, but the human worker took me away from my boy.

"Oh no, what was she doing?" I wondered surprisingly when gently she placed a collar of shimmery cobalt around my scruff. The *sign* to let everyone know that I had been selected!

"I had a new home! I had a new home!" I wanted to shout to the highest of the heavens as I snuggled back into the arms of my boy. I was so excited I peed on him, but he didn't mind.

He just shrugged his shoulders and said, "It probably won't be the last time!" I couldn't wait to get back to my mama and tell her the wonderful news I had been selected! I was special!

"See you in a few weeks, Little Boy!" I shouted as he exited the door.

Ahhh, those extraordinary memories . . . I love this life!

My Kitty-Brothers!

I recall letting you know that one of my most beloved parts of the day is when we all gather on Big D and Nee Nee's bed at sleep time to cuddle inside the coverings and hang out together.

It is at this special time that one of my humans will take advantage of these moments to engage in story time. This is when I get to hear about moments in the life of my humans as well as chronicles about me before my memory had taken hold. Some of the stories warm my heart, but there are some accounts that also make me a tad sad.

The stories that make me melancholy are the accounts when one of them begins to talk about my kitty-brothers, whom I barely remember but feel their presence in my being, Tigger Magoo and Ginger Roozer.

I have to laugh when I hear the story of how my humans prepared my four-legged felines for my arrival into the household. From what I hear, they'd say, "A Hurricane is a brewin' so be prepared!" or at times, "Here comes a Hurricane . . . get ready!"

I seriously don't know what all the fuss was about because from my point of view, I'm SURE that they couldn't wait for my appearance in the house. Who wouldn't?

I'm positive you are aware of the old dog-cat relationship, that cats don't like dogs and all dogs do is chase the cats, blah, blah, blah. Well, in this case I guess it is true.

At the moment I entered into my new house, I spotted Tigger Magoo peering around the corner with his carroty-colored hackles standing straight on end. I wanted to talk about this, you know, man-to-man so I approached him and talkin' about rude!

He hissed at me complete with baring teeth, and when I went to apologize with a nose-to-nose greeting, well, he hit me! That rascal who was no bigger than a flea reached out with his paw and hit me!

OUCH! He smacked me right across my face. How do you like that for a warm greeting and welcome to the house!

But I was NOT about to give up, so as he turned to walk away I gave chase to him, which is when I realized what a great race track I was going to have in my new home. The hallway circulates through five rooms, and one could run laps without ever having a door closed in their face.

I trailed him until he ran up some stairs. I was only a little guy back then and my eight-week-old legs didn't know how to navigate stairs, so I feigned disinterest! Yep, I let him get away, just this once.

Ginger Roozer, rightfully named, is the other orange-tinted tabby. He was a bit braver and had quite the dignity for a cat. He sauntered toward me with his tail held high as if to let me know he was NOT going to be pushed around.

Just being in his presence prompted me to sit on my haunches and show patience for our formal meeting. Ginger Roozer didn't hesitate to approach me and parked a foot from my muzzle. He looked intently into my eyes, mesmerizing me with his confidence not only in himself but the assuredness that stated who the master was in this house it certainly wouldn't be me!

Okay then . . . I can respect that!

And I did . . . our pecking order stayed true to form from that first day forward. I made it my mission to distress the skittish Tigger, and boy, torment I did! When I became big enough to take the helm regarding the stairs, I chased Tigger up and down, in and out, over and under.

For a small thing, he is extremely speedy. He thought he'd outsmart me by jumping high onto a chair or counter, and I have to admit, that was a pretty good alternative since I am more earthbound than my feline brother.

However, that made me even more eager to nip at his mitts or bite at the tip of his tail. He'd return the favor by swatting me on the top of the head with his paw as he spat at me. I could not let a day pass without my quest to antagonize my four-legged brother at the top of my to-do list!

Ginger, on the other hand, well, we had an unspoken understanding that he was not to be engaged in such childish antics. He perched himself on the dining room chairs or on the bed, and while I approached I entered his boundary with admiration and caution. I was calmed and comforted by his presence and took that opportunity to settle close by for my naps as are needed by youngsters such as myself.

Sir Walter Scott once said, "Cats are a mysterious kind of folk. There is more passing in their minds than we are aware." I couldn't agree more, Mr. Scott. I couldn't agree more.

In the meantime, I'll continue to have Tigger Magoo as my playmate and Ginger Roozer as my regal guardian. I love this life . . .

Little D

I owe a lot to Little Daddy in view of the fact that he did in fact choose me to be a member of this family. It was also his ingenious thinking that granted me the name of *Hurricane*. Let me tell you how the story begins.

When he was just a sprite in Ohio, his most beloved movies were *Air Bud* stories. Nee Nee told me he watched them time and again and dreamed of having a golden retriever like me. When he was told the family was relocating to North Carolina, they promised they would locate a house with a large fenced-in back yard so he could own a dog.

Little D decided early on, even before the official move, that if his dog was a boy he'd name it Hurricane and if it was a girl, he'd name it Goldie. Therefore, before I was even a consideration, I was lovingly referred to as "HG" . . . aaaahhh that sounds nice!

I never tire of hearing Little D tell that story. I guess you could say our special connection began even before I was officially adopted. But the bond continues as a result of all the activities we do together.

Little Daddy and I have been playing soccer together since I was just a teeny-weeny one. So whenever he says, "Come on, Hurricane, let's go play soccer!" I just get all energized inside. And really what it amounts to is a glorified match of "keep away" because that's what he does or at least tries to do, keep the ball away from me.

But I show him, and I wrap my legs around that ball and hold on for dear life. "Okay, Little D, I got you now!" as the ball sails over my head through the air. Darn, missed again!

There are a multitude of things Little D and I do that make our relationship special. We play wrestle mania, and he gets these big overstuffed gloves out of the closet and puts them on. Then he slaps them together and dares me to charge at him. It's great fun trying to retrieve those gloves off his fingers.

We get yelled at sometimes, "Watch out for that TV you guys!"

"Yeah, yeah, Big D. Got it!" I cast his way because I know Little D and I are just getting warmed up.

Next, we run through the house and I attempt to track him down and get those gloves off his hands. I lunge at his britches and he tumbles to the floor and laughs and giggles, which is such a wonderful sound to my ears. Little D is in hysterics as I nip at his feet and try to take his socks off while he's scampering through the house.

"Oh Little D, I almost got you that time!" The challenge is trying to get my feet to stop on the hardwood floors; it's like wheels on ice.

There are moments when I forget I'm stronger than Little D, and I lunge or grip too hard and he gets frustrated with me and says, "Hurricane, I'm done, I quit!" But I really don't mean it.

"I'm sorry Little D, really I am," I say as I flop onto the floor and hang my head. I just forget my size. I would never hurt Little D, he's my boy!

But I must say, out of all the times we spend with each other the absolute best time is when we cuddle together. I lie in his lap and he always has that warm touch which reminds me he will not leave me.

Hah, I wanted to say now that I'm too big for his lap, but really I don't think I'll ever be too big for his lap because I **still** try to snuggle into his lap for an embrace. "Hurricane, you are not small anymore," he tells me although he still finds a way for me to settle into his legs or close beside him.

I get comfortable and begin to close my eyes when Little D will say, "Awww Hurricane, you're my boy!" to which I respond.

"Yeah, Little D, you're my boy too!"

I love this life . . .

Offspring!

Let's see, what is it called when parents have six kids?

Sextuplets? Yeah! Well, that's what I had.

Well no, I didn't actually have them and wouldn't want to mislead you into thinking I did all the work; Sadie did. Sadie was the golden retriever I was bred with, which is the formal way of saying, "One and done!" like Big D so casually calls it.

It started like this . . . my parents know her parents and they thought it was a good idea to breed us and sell the puppies. Well that's fine and dandy, but I was just a smidgen of a dog at the time and had no idea what I was doing.

Heavens to Betsy, Sadie had to teach me *EVERY-THING* and I don't know about you but that certainly hurt **MY** male ego. Isn't the "man" supposed to be the smooth and debonair one? At least that's what I'd been told anyway, although I'm sure I was anything BUT charming!

On top of that, it was truly a rush job, and I don't intend for that to be mean or disrespectful, but here's what happened. Sadie's family was driving to Texas for the holidays, so they had a plethora of things to do before they left on their trip the next morning—so much for wining-and-dining and romance!

Anyway, they dropped Sadie off and our human folk put us in our fenced back yard. For goodness sake, she kept getting real close to me and tried to climb on my back when I just wanted to play.

"Come on, Sadie, let's go get the ball!"

We played this game from side to side and back and forth. She kept giving me directions by moving me hither and yon, and after about an hour and a half (what can I say, I'm "slow")

I got it! Except then, right there in front of God and everyone, we were . . . stuck! I couldn't get loose and of all places, we weren't anywhere private; we were in the middle of our deck! Seriously?

Big D and Nee Nee kept looking out the back window, and when we finally were unattached I wanted to go in the house and be by myself.

Actually, what I really wanted was to be given a bath; yeah, me wanting a bath. Sadie's family finally came and got her and then I never saw her again . . . well geez, that's kind of impersonal, isn't it?

Two pages on the calendar were turned when my family got all excited and began shouting.

"We have puppies! Six puppies!"

We? Don't you mean me?

Little D danced around and said, "Hurricane, you are a Daddy!"

Really?

Gosh, don't know how that came to be but, nonetheless, the family was happy so I guess it's a good thing. I danced with them around the living room and pretended to be excited.

They made phone calls and Big D and Nee Nee patted each the other on the back, congratulating each other saying how they were grandparents now. This is all too confusing for me so I let them carry on. I went about my business and found a nice, soft spot on the carpet and closed my eyes.

I don't know what all this excitement is about but hey, I love this life . . .

Helping Big D!

I take great pride in being man's best friend and doing the job I was born to do . . . *whatever* that may entail!

Come to think about it, though, I don't think I've read the manual yet. Perhaps that is why I always seem to be getting in trouble.

Sometimes I am pretty good at it and other times, oh well, we can't all be perfect, right?!

I feel it is my utmost responsibility to bring cheer and happiness to the family and help out as much as I can, and I always try to be prepared to do whatever is asked of me.

This much I know . . . most every morning begins with an identical routine; the first glimpses of light from the exterior put me in action to vault onto the bed and bestow licky-lickies on Big Daddy's face and in his ear. He rapidly rolls onto his side or belly and pulls the covers over his head. "Hurricane, STOP!" he grumbles to me in his mad voice.

I quickly bring him to laughter by rubbing my neck and nuzzle on his face and plopping down on top of him. I know this makes him happy that I help him get out of bed, and in spite of the grumbling he rises and lumbers downstairs to make coffee. He says he might as well get up and run since I've woken him—see, I told you I was helpful!

Next, Big D wraps himself in his running gear. He gathers his socks and shoes and I try to assist him by intertwining in his feet pulling on the laces to make sure they are nice and tight. "Hurricane, you goofy dog, let me tie my shoes!" he tells me.

I follow him around the house like a tail follows a dog, but he doesn't ever take me with him although I try to be included. The one time I did get to go running with him I saw this big green garbage can and I was afraid it would attack Big D, so I pranced on my hind legs with my paws on his chest to push him out of the way.

I not only wanted to save him from harm, but I also didn't want Big D to be offended by all the collections of doggie doo-doo in there. He never took me again!

So now my aid really begins when he arrives back home; he is all wet with stinky moisture on his skin. That's when I know it is my turn; for the reason we begin this routine that simply sends me over the moon.

Big D walks over to the stairs and stretches his foot onto the third or fourth step, and I'm invited to sit beside his leg while he does his leg stretches. I try to encourage him as best I can, but I get so inundated with licking all the sweat off that I sometimes forget to throw out those supportive responses. I've slurped so much moisture he doesn't even need to take a shower before work, I'm certain!

But it doesn't end there, No Sireee!

My next job is to sit with Big D while he puts an ice bag on his knee. Big D says he's getting too old for this, whatever "this" is . . . which I don't see what that has to do with getting ice, which is one of my favorite treats by the way, and he puts it on his knee?

How gross!

Don't expect me to eat one of those when you're done with them.

On days Big D stays home, it's CUDDLE TIME!!!

This is the best part of all and I do NOT mind helping with this, truly my pleasure!

Big D says he needs to relax and unwind, thus he basks in the morning sunbeams that radiate brightly through the front door window. He settles in while I gently remind him to make room for me! Ahhh, this helping stuff is such hard work, but someone's got to do it!

"Thanks, Mr. Magoo, I don't know what I'd do without you!" he says.

See, I told you I'm helpful . . . I love this life . . .

Welcome Home!

After being chosen by my boy on that fateful day in November, the day I was to be taken home couldn't get here fast enough. Every day was spent badgering my mama with questions she couldn't possibly know the answer to such as, "When am I going to my new home?"

"Do you think I'll like my new family?"

Or the one that made both of us a little sad, "Will I ever get to see you again, Mama?"

She would soothingly nudge me and gently place a licky-licky on my nose as if to say she couldn't answer my complex wonderings. What I would soon realize is that having a new boy and a new home was a mixed bag as I began the difficult proceedings of saying goodbye one at a time to all my brothers and sisters.

But most of all, the more complicated maneuver was leaving my mama. No one had prepared me for the heartbreaking procedures of a final farewell.

One by one, the human families of my siblings arrived, which always began a similar chain of actions; claim their chosen one, take them to the sink for their earliest water bath, dry the coat with the aid of a blower, and be held in their new family's arms.

Ahhh, when was my boy coming so I could be swaddled and cuddled into his caring limbs?

Until it was my turn, I could only imagine as I lovingly bid a warm departure to my kinfolk catapulting them into their fresh journey.

"Take good care of yourself there, Bro. I'll always think of you!" or "Hey Sis, we had such great times, didn't we? Have a blessed life! I'll miss you!"

One early Saturday morning in December as the sun was perched on top of the barren trees, my time had arrived; my new family sauntered through the door with a skipping boy in the lead. I was captivated by the excitement, yet a tugging of my heart strings began as a momentary look over my shoulder caught the glimpse of my mama.

She displayed a courageous exterior but the sorrow in her eyes shone through as separately and one by one, her children were departing.

I nuzzled with my tether to the universe and whispered, "Goodbye, Mama. I'll always love you . . . thank you for the opportunity to be in this world and to live my life with my new family."

My mama hoisted me into the arms of the human worker as she bid me farewell as only a mother could do with the parting words; "Be good now, you hear? And make me proud! I love you!"

The leaving routine commenced, although I didn't like the water element and was thoroughly thankful when the blowing ceased. I thought perhaps I'd be propelled to my new home with the force of that current of air upon me. As my humans jostled into a contraption called a car, my boy enveloped me in a welcoming, cozy covering which warmed my moist fur.

I dozed on the ride home so I couldn't tell you the time or distance it took us to get there.

"We're here, Hurricane!" my boy proudly bellowed. He carried me out of the car and placed me on this scratchy brownish-green poky stuff that hurt my tender feet. Then he pleaded with me to potty.

Really? After all those weeks peeing on newsprint and now you want me to do that on this prickly russet stuff?

Well, if you insist. Besides, I really did have to go after that long excursion. Their shrieking scared the bee-jeebies out of me and I stopped when they all started whooping and hollering, "Good boy, Hurricane! You went potty!"

"Well, Geez Louise guys, it's a natural bodily function. Besides, I did what you told me to do. I AM a pretty smart boy if I do say so myself!" I threw their way.

The rest of the day was spent playing, cuddling, loving, and laughing and of course, pottying . . . there really was so much to learn!

Little D tenderly carried me in his arms and murmured into my ear, "Welcome home, Hurricane, Welcome home!"

Ahhh, I love this life . . .

Facts of Five!

My Nee Nee has a blog and one of the columns she writes is called "Facts of Five." I'll do my best to explain the principle. She teaches children with special needs, and with one of her groups she would have calendar time and close the morning with this activity.

She would present to the children a category such as Five Cartoons and they'd name five cartoons, or "five items to eat on your pizza" and the class would make a list of five foods. The students had to consider and name ideas that fit each group. She thought it was fun, engaging, and she was able to get to know her students by the information they presented.

Well, I liked the idea so I thought perhaps it was a good format to use to give you five additional facts about me. You already know the basic things, like I'm a dog and my name is Hurricane.

My family also tells me I have a pretty posh life—do you think so? Maybe you shouldn't answer that question as it may incriminate me.

So anyway, here I go: Facts of Five and things you may or may not know about me yet!

1. *I am afraid of the dark.*

Okay, laugh all you want, but I looked it up on the Internet and it's very real. They, whoever *they* are, call it nyctophobia and did you know it is pretty common among young children?

Yeah, I know I'm a dog and not a young child, but seriously, I think this applies. Anyway, when it is dark outside and I have to go potty, usually before bedtime or even in the morning if the sun hasn't risen yet, I make someone go out with me and go down the deck stairs before I will use the bathroom.

Now, when I say I "make" them go outside, what I mean by that is I sit and stare at them and refuse to budge until someone makes a motion to actually descend the set of steps with me. Our backyard is vast and packed with numerous tall trees and a creek bed, so one can never tell what lies within.

So, I hesitate and stare until they stand in protection while I do my business.

Lights, you ask? Nope, not enough. I need my family to accompany me to the ball, so to speak.

2. *I crave attention.*

So when I want my people's attention, I resort to a very tried-and-true trick in my bag; I find their belongings and carry them downstairs into the living room, our gathering place. We have an oak, rectangular coffee table in front of the Carolina blue couch, and anything that is vulnerable to my finding gets put in my favorite place.

It IS my ultimate favorite downstairs hiding place because I just fit under the table and they can't get to me there unless they move the platform.

AHHH, I got them there. I've been known to take plant leaves from Big D's inside vegetation under there . . . ooohhh, that makes him mad and that is when he reverts to name-calling like *Devil-Dog!*

Sometimes I'll take tissues or paper towels from the garbage can to my favorite spot, or shoes—anything, like I said, to get their attention.

Is it worth the scolding? Sure it is . . .

3. *I am relentless.*

I will prod and persuade until I get what I want whether it be a caress on my ear or someone to play with. Call me stubborn, but hey, a man has to do what a man has to do. In this case, a dog has to do . . .

If I want to be patted on my head, I will hassle my humans by getting so close they must fall over me to move. If they are sitting I will attempt to slide onto their laps and give them licky-lickies on their face. If I'm standing next to one of my family, I'll lean into them almost knocking them down with my strength. I will position my snout on their hand or give them sloppy-slurps on their fingers to achieve my goal.

I really have no shame when it comes to accomplishing my objective at hand. Lucky me though, I don't often have to resort to these antics but again, a dog has to do what a dog has to do.

4. *I love to go on walks.*

I know, what dog doesn't, you ask. But this time is exceptional because I get to visit via urine and smell; sorry if you think that's gross but I am a dog, you know. I get to experience which of my buddies has been through the area or who yet has to take a walk.

These goings-on are typically led by Big D, but sometimes Little D will ride his scooter and then we have loads of fun playing chase. But this moment in my day reminds me that there is a world out there bigger than that which occurs inside my very own house.

While I am unique, I am one of many, which is a nice reminder when I tend to get selfish and want the world to revolve around my wants and needs.

But then again, who am I fooling. It SHOULD orbit around me—I AM the dog!

5. *I have a set bedtime.*

I become extremely fidgety and restless near 9:00 or 9:30 p.m. It's difficult for me to "settle down," like Big D suggests, until we all head upstairs, get our jammies on— well, they get their PJ's on—and we inhabit the big doggie bed known as Big D and Nee Nee's divan.

It is such a treat to have us all come together on the bed snuggling within the warm, cozy covers. My humans read separate books or Big D will read aloud to Little D but whatever it is they are doing, the important thing is, **we** gather.

That is so special to me, and it reminds me that at the end of each day I have many blessings in my life—first and foremost, my family.

Play Time!

At 8:00 or 8:30 in the evening, I get my second wind and in my opinion, that is the ultimate time to play!

What **IS** unfortunate about this time period is that it is near or around the time my family sits down to rest and relax from their day.

Thus far, they've come home from their work or school place, prepared and finished dinner; my humans have cleaned up. They have organized and packed lunches for the next day. Nee Nee has prepared lessons for her children, made necessary phone calls to parents, and logged on to that box with all the letter keys and the screen that shows all my pictures and stories.

"Yeah, she knows they're there. I was busted a long time ago." Big D has helped Little D with his social studies or math homework, and we've endured the practicing of that crazy black tube that bursts out whacky sounds.

Over and done with getting their outside coverings chosen and ironed for the next work day AND they've already fed and taken me for my jaunt around the neighborhood to visit my friends.

So do you think it is too much to ask to play with me?

I certainly don't think so but, apparently, they do at times.

However, being the persevering dog that I am, I will go to extreme measures to entice one of my humans to get involved with my playtime. I do this by visiting my toy-box and one by one, I chose my poison, promenade to someone and deposit the preferred item, perhaps Mr. Rabbit or Mr. Cow, at their feet.

I sit, I stare, and I wait!

If no one responds, I repeat the process of selecting a different play thing from my container; maybe Mr. Pig will get their attention. I proudly stroll to yet another person and drop it in front of them.

Again . . . I sit, I stare, and I wait!

Sometimes I even go so far as to ease the elected item onto their lap, possibly a gooey raw hide, and then I go into my "I sit, I stare, and I wait" routine.

All I get is a "OHH gross, Hurricane!" What about these procedures do they not understand?

Well, when they are being emphatically stubborn, I must resort to . . . yep, you guessed it; fetching socks. I go on a "search and seizure" for my human's socks that have yet to make it to the laundry basket. Being the busy people they are, I usually find one lying around somewhere.

So I strut with the foot covering snugly in my mouth to the front of the talking box, and I lie down so they can observe what I'm giving my attention to. I also make sure my face is toward them so I can see and anticipate their next move.

Then I start.

I start chewing AND biting AND stretching, which leads to ripping AND tearing into shreds.

I repeat this process as often as is necessary because what I have come to learn is that ONE of them will eventually say, "Okay Hurricane, let's play!"

Ahhh, music to my ears . . . Typically, I don't even have to get that far because when the sock is drooping from my jowls, they lunge toward me to capture their prized possession.

They proceed to get on the floor complete with the mention that is it nearly 8:30 and I SHOULD be getting ready for bed, but naaah, I'd rather play! . . . and PLAY!

This is really what I wanted the entire time. I just wonder why it takes them so long to get the message.

I love this life . . .

Visitation!

Envision me being in a position of having visitation rights with my children. Remember I told you I had six pups, well, not me, but Sadie.

Anyway, I'm glad to report all our pups were chosen and placed into good homes but two pups continue to live in my neighborhood so I am allotted visitation with them every once in a while.

I must admit, I enjoy seeing the children and catching up with their families. I like knowing how life is going for them and what's happening in their world because we often get so busy with our own lives we just miss out on the little things. It's also rewarding to see what fine pups they are becoming.

So, you can imagine my delight when I had my first visit with Savannah and Logan. Boy, they sure are cute! I guess those adorable, charming young ones do resemble me. I mustn't say that too loud because their mother Sadie joined us for the day, and I don't mean any disregard to their mama.

Anyway, here in North Carolina our summer days get to be pretty hot, and on this particular day it was a steamy one-hundred-plus degrees.

When those children came into our fence they began hopping all over me, darting around the yard, bouncing on top of each other and wrestling each other to the ground.

They continually covered the face of their mother with licky-lickies and slobbering slurps.

When they finished showering her, they did the same with me. Come on guys, really, is this necessary?

Sadie looked tired, but I guess being four weeks out of giving up the six young 'uns she's allowed to be a tad bit exhausted. Those wee ones ran us over the entire yard; jumping on our backs, passing the ball to us so they could play fetch, hurdling over us, specifically our faces when we stopped a moment to catch our breath.

They were so energetic and relentless. Heavens, I don't know where they get all that energy from, probably their mother! If I had an ounce of that get-up-and-go those kids did . . . ahhh, to be young again!

By time an hour or so rolled away, Sadie and I glanced at each other as we drank from the water bowls our owners set before us, both as if to say, "Are we done yet?"

I love my children but I'm far too old for all this engagement in recreation and amusement, especially in this heat. We were sucking air, so we sat in the shade and the kids gathered around. It was enjoyable to witness what they were becoming. I watched with a compassionate eye and silently hoped they were minding their manners, listening to the expectations and wishes of their human family.

Out of respect, I chose to remain hushed on the lecturing front.

The visitation with my brood brought to mind an ancient Chinese proverb which states, "To understand your parents' love, you must raise children yourself."

Perhaps it is with this visit, that I finally do understand my mama's love. I comprehend it at a deeper level, but know that in order to do right by my offspring; I must love them unconditionally and honor the human relatives of each to do what is right by them.

It is with this final contemplation that I sent them on their way with fine wishes knowing they are in homes filled with commitment, sacrifice, and love.

However, they are also going home with a great deal of sweat and slobber situated on their coat as well. Glad I could leave a legacy.

I love this life . . .

SNOW!!!

North Carolina isn't known for getting a lot of snow, so imagine my surprise when I woke up one morning, stepped on the back deck to go potty and there was this white stuff all over the deck and the yard.

What in the world?

I'm a fall pup born in the month of October, so I'm already prone to liking the cooler weather. When the days become cooler, especially for our walks in the evening, I feel so frisky and lighthearted I get the urge to kick up my heels. But this was even better.

On this specific day there was exhilaration in the air. Little D was born in Ohio so while he is used to the fluffy mashed-potato flakes, he welcomed the snowflakes layering the ground. He was set to spend the day sledding and snowboarding but decided to play with me first.

"You da' Man, Little D!"

He bundled up in mismatched clothes that covered every portion of his skin. If I hadn't been able to smell, I wouldn't have known Little D was encased in all that material because I sure couldn't see him except for his eyes.

We toddled onto the driveway and he threw my worn, green tennis ball across the yard. "Hey, where did it go? Little D, I think those white particles just ate my ball!"

I sprinted across the yard and let my nose do the work . . . now where is that ball?

Here it is! Hey Little D, this is fun playing hide-n-seek with the ball!

We continued to scamper about and wrestle each other to the ground. I thought I was strong but Little D was a good match since the snow was slick and I couldn't get my footing.

Little D began throwing snowballs at me, so I got him by burying my muzzle into the snow, raising my head to flick it into the air, snow particles falling on top of him. He laughed as I rolled onto my back to kick the stuff toward his face. He thought I was making a snow angel. I don't know about that, but this sure felt good on the fur.

We did extensive playing that day, and I was dog tired when he wanted me to climb aboard his sled to go for a ride. I wasn't that daring so I plopped in the white matter and refused to move.

"I'm weary, Little D—but boy, this sure was fun! Let's do this again tomorrow!"

I love this life . . .

Christmas!

"Oh Christmas tree, oh Christmas tree, how lovely are your branches and your sparkling blue lights and your ornaments and the attractive burgundy ribbons that dangle from your boughs."

WHOA! . . . when my humans put up this lovely ever-green tree in our living room, my first thought was "what the heck!" because I wasn't quite sure what the point was.

Then Little D told me that Christmas was a holiday where the birth of Jesus Christ was celebrated.

Wow! Someone else is having a birthday like I did. I asked Little D if we could take Jesus to DQ for ice cream, but he just smiled, patted me on the head, and said that He wasn't alive anymore. Rather, Jesus was in a special place called Heaven waiting for those who have yet to die.

I really don't understand the meaning of this holiday but even so, the tree is quite exquisite.

The tree glimmered with sapphire lights in the darkened room. Big D sat on the floor leaning against the couch while gawking up at the glowing showpiece. I curled up between his legs and rested my head on his thigh: this action seems to encourage story time as well as gentle strokes upon my head.

I truly wanted to hear and understand this holiday. But rather than delve into why the celebration was sacred, he let me know he felt a sense of sadness this season, regardless of the joyful illusion. I wanted to hear more so I met his eyes to signal my interest so he'd go on with his speaking.

He murmured softly into the air, and I felt his sorrow as he tenderly caressed my ears, my face. He began: "Last year, Hurricane, you were just a little guy and it was your first Christmas. Your kitty-brother Ginger would race through the remnants of torn paper and empty boxes littering the floor in the family room aside the tree enticing you to chase him. Ginger would hide under a pile of brightly colored wrapping and peer through an opening to watch you approach and then he'd bound out and the chase would be set in motion once more. Christmas had brought him the gift of youthfulness. It was a splendid day!"

I continued to listen to Big D's reminiscing words. "Tragedy struck the next evening. Ginger Roozer wanted to go for his nightly scouring of the neighborhood. After a couple hours when he hadn't appeared at the door, Nee Nee went out in search for the plump, ginger feline.

"After ignored attempts at calling him, she walked the perimeter of the house and was startled by a delicate whimper. She faced the sound and found Ginger Roozer lying in the pine straw next to the steps. He gazed up at her with pleading frightened eyes. Hurricane, Nee Nee says she will never forget the terrified alarmed look on his face."

I was captivated by Big D's words and feared the ending, although I thought he needed to tell his story so I allowed him to continue. "Nee Nee called him and he gave a faint meow as if to beg for help. Ginger was unable to move so she ran into the house for a towel and yelled out that something had happened to Ginger. I ran outside on the porch and called him to come to me but he was unable to move. Nee Nee scooped him in her arms and after frantic calls to locate an open emergency veterinarian clinic we were off.

"The drive to the vet hospital felt like an eternity, and we were greeted by the receptionist at the door. She seized the bundle that held Ginger. We sat frenzied, awaiting any news on our beloved pet."

The doctor came to us with the grim news; my kitty-brother had been shot with a BB gun. A pellet entered his back and hit directly on the spine, paralyzing him. "The most humane thing to do for our boy was to have him put to sleep rather than to live a life of misery and prolonged pain."

My heart broke for my kitty-brother Ginger. Being a babyish sprite of ten weeks, I was so wrapped up in my own being I hadn't picked up on the sadness of my human family. I was really sorry.

I felt Big D's grief. I licked Big D's hand to pass along my sympathies. I also had a powerful longing to take away his pain. After such a personal loss is that even possible?

Cuddling with Big D, I couldn't help but remind him of a quote I once heard by Chief Seattle: "There is no death, only a change of worlds."

I wanted to reassure Big D that Ginger Roozer was no longer with our family in our world, but in the Heaven-world with Jesus. As we speak, Ginger is racing after a catnip mouse across the mounds of vibrantly decorated package wrap.

The thought forced a smile to my heart as the lights flickered on the branches.

"...thinking of you too Ginger Roozer, thinking of you, too!"

Stuffed Children of Little D!

No, I know what you're thinking, but this isn't about my own children but the one-hundred-and-thirty-plus children of my boy, Little D. He has been collecting his "children" as he calls them since he was a belly baby. That's what he refers to himself when he was in Nee Nee's belly.

I guess I was a belly baby once too!

Anyway, my boy has an entire closet overflowing with his plush friends, which he lovingly refers to as the hotel, so all the children can be housed and engage in recreation. In the corner of his room, its heaped high with stuffed pals created after a dog-pile was set in motion after winning an imaginary football game.

Let's see, there's a giraffe with a blue bottom. Evidently, when he was a little bitty boy of two, Big D and Nee Nee were painting the living room so Little D thought he and his friend could help. So he dipped the muted-colored patchwork animal into the paint, hence his name, Giraffey with a Blue Bottom!

Then there's Arty who is wearing a T-shirt displaying a picture that my boy drew when he was in third grade.

Who could forget, Dippy, the multicolored rabbit; Dallas, named for the place he was purchased; and Lemon Drop since he is the color of, well, a lemon drop.

There's Moon-Bear, Vanilla, Mr. Dragon, Paloma, and Boxer Bear, all complete with a tale lovingly relayed by my boy.

Little Daddy has a plethora of children that envelop his bed. Big D says there's hardly a place for Little D to sleep, which is probably why I never get to sleep in Little D's room. But Clementine, Rainbow Bear, Fenway, Mimsy, Daisy-Girl, Vernon all have the opportunity to curl up with him to sleep.

My boy declares he can't choose a most beloved because you can't prefer one of your children over another, which is why he rotates the brood every couple of weeks so they can take turns making memories.

But, do you want to know which one is my favorite?

All of them!

Yep, that's right; Chirpy, Molly Bear, Big Bird . . . all or any I can get my jowls on at any given moment.

Sometimes I think it is my mission in life to terrorize those lovely creatures. It's the same procedure I use to fetch socks, the old "snatch and grab" technique. I wait for the childproof gate to be put aside, which was put there for the specific reason of protecting ME from them—or is it the other way around, protecting them from ME? Anyway, the removal of this shield for some reason or another allows me to dart in and grab one of the children, or as many that I can fit into my mouth. I've even been known to take those stuffed ones that belong to my boy's friends. Once I took Mr. Wuf, an N.C. State Wolfpack mascot; something just told me that Mr. Wuf wouldn't get along well with Ramses, Little D's Carolina companion.

In any case, when one or two get captured, I take it to one of my favorite hiding places and just gnaw on that soft fur to infiltrate it with my slobber. I give the beast a few shakes of my head to roughen it up a bit and create a matted look to its covering fresh with drool.

Oh yeah, I like the ears best because they fit easily into my oral cavity, and then there are the paws, those fit nicely into the orifice too!

My objective in this endeavor is merely to have fun with one of my brothers or sisters since I rarely get the chance. But there have been times when I shake one too many and a lone thread becomes a hole, a hole becomes a tear and the tear becomes a . . . OOOPS!

All of a sudden, stuffing is filling my mouth and haphazardly overflows onto the floor. Oh no, its guts are escaping!

I act quickly since it won't be long until I'm busted! I retreat to one of my sleeping spots and feign innocence. Then someone says, "HURR-I-CANE!" or "Hurricane Scott Spaine" . . . wasn't aware a middle name was given to me until my humans are livid with me!

Little D rushes to the victim—uhh, I mean, his child—and yells for Nee Nee. If my capture has a cut, it may need to be taken to the *hossible*; the word my boy use to call the hospital, or that perhaps it now needs a bath. HEE HEE!!

This little escapade sets off quite the reaction. Ahhh, sometimes things get too quiet around here and it is required of me to stir things up a bit even if my reputation of being man's best friend is in jeopardy.

But not for long, as they tend to be very forgiving. Nee Nee says that someday Little D will outgrow his children, but I don't think so. That tender-hearted, loyal boy will cherish us all forever; he may grow up, but he certainly won't outgrow love.

I love this life . . .

Road Kill!

No, silly, not THAT kind; not where carcasses of mashed up animals on the road that got run over by God knows what and their remnants are stretched over the pavement in shards of blush. UGH! Just thinking of that makes my belly twist and turn upside down like the particles sifting through an hourglass.

I know this because whenever my family gets in the automobile to go somewhere and I happen to be invited, Little D, Nee Nee or Big D will voice "UGH, that poor animal!" which of course forces me to look at what they are pointing out because I'm just nosey like that, and gross, just gross!

I remind myself that I must be very careful around vehicles so I don't end up as *Road Kill*.

Anyway, I'm getting a bit sidetracked as I have a tendency to do. One day Little D and Nee Nee had gone on a shopping expedition and returned with this, well, this thing that was flat with ne'er an ounce of innards. It was covered with bristly, gray-and-white-meshed pelt stripes with only two arms! Really? I thought raccoons had four arms so I couldn't help wondering what happened to his other arms . . . bless his heart!

However, he had such a cute face with guess what? Yep, a squeaker in his nose! Oh, that made me as happy as shark on a feeding frenzy!

The second most excellent part? He has an extra squeaker in his elongated, colorless tail . . . two squeakers! I don't know what I ever did to deserve this new plaything, but it was fabulous!

Nee Nee and Little D fooled around with me for what seemed like hours tossing it, and I'd go chase Mr. Raccoon and eventually plop myself on the floor to drive them mad with continually chewing on the squeaker, hee hee! Oh Mr. R, that seemed like a fine name for him.

Well, then Big D came home and I brought Mr. R to meet him at the door. I wanted to tell Big D all about Mr. R, but was highly offended when Big D spotted him on the hardwood with his body twisted and his legs and tail sprawled in various directions. His poor head was laying flat and his tongue spewed out, and Big D pegged him as *Road Kill.*

Uhhh, I'm so offended. That's not nice, Big D, to call my friend a name, especially with such a gross correlation. UGH!!!

Nonetheless, despite the given name of Mr. R, he has become one of my cherished companions. I carry him around in my chops like a toddler with a security blanket.

Perhaps I've found my solution to being by myself in the shadowy house?

I know Road Kill, uh, Mr. R will look after me!

I love this life . . .

Memories!

Awww, looking back I sure was a cute endearing little bugger, wasn't I?

I can't quite recall what drove me to climb into the dryer that day, but I do remember feeling such smugness at my triumph. Perhaps it was to liberate one of those socks I am so captivated by.

I think as we grow older—yeah, I know, I'm such an old rascal at a mere two years old—however, at any age, we are given the opportunity to glance back on life, to ponder and reflect on specific moments and to gain an understanding that life's lessons have bestowed on us by this universe in which we live. A number of experiences may bring a chuckle to our hearts while others bring us to a standstill.

It is a conglomeration of those encounters that we christen this thing called *Life*!

Life through the Eyes of a Hurricane chronicles these events that paint the canvas of my existence be it exciting, mundane and otherwise.

I have such wonderful astonishing memories and you know what? There are more to come because I just was informed the other day that we are adopting a new member of the family.

Remember I told you about my kitty-brother, Ginger-Roozer, and the ordeal my family went through after his senseless death? Well, it seems that while Nee Nee and Little D sought after and desired another kitty awfully bad, Big D just couldn't bring himself to get emotionally involved with another pet. He just wasn't prepared to offer his heart and spirit to one more soul, and who could fault him for the self-preservation?

However, I've learned with love comes great sacrifice, and Big D has given the go ahead to get another kitty.

So it is with this blessing that the search is launched for a feline fuzz-ball.

WHEW . . . WHEW!!!

Let the fun begin . . .

CPSIA information can be obtained at www.ICGtesting.com
Printed in the USA
BVOW071623300112

281665BV00004B/1/P